P9-AOF-607

Praise for John Powell's books

"John Powell's bestsellers are more vital, appealing, and readable than ever."
—*Theological Book Service*

"Love is the motivating force in Powell's life. Mention the word to him in casual conversation, and he'll talk till dawn."
—*William Griffin*

"Powell makes it possible to change oneself and live a life of love and understanding."
—*Haddonfield, NJ*

"Powell's books embody these words: 'In order to know how to live, you must know how to love.'"
—*North Royalton, OH*

"John Powell writes for people of all ages."
—*Palm Coast, FL*

"Powell's books are timeless. They are like old friends you haven't seen for years."
—*Franksville, WI*

The Challenge of

FAITH

The Challenge of
FAITH

John Powell

ThomasMore®
– An RCL Company –

Allen, Texas

Copyright © 1998 John Powell

All rights reserved. No part of this book shall be
reproduced or transmitted in any form or by any means,
electronic or mechanical, including photocopying,
recording, or by any information or retrieval system,
without written permission from the Publisher.

Send all inquiries to:
Thomas More®
An RCL Company
200 East Bethany Drive
Allen, Texas 75002–3804

Toll Free   800–264–0368
Fax   800–688–8356

Visit our website at **www.rclweb.com**

Printed in the United States of America

Library of Congress Catalog Card Number: 98–60969

7425   ISBN 0–88347–425–5

1 2 3 4 5   02 01 00 99 98

CONTENTS

Be patient toward all that is unsolved
in your heart . . .
Try to love the questions themselves . . .
Do not seek the answers
    which cannot be given
    because you would not be able
    to live them.
And the point is,
    to live everything.

Live the questions now.
Perhaps you will then
    gradually,
    without noticing it,
    Live along some distant day
    into the answers.

Rainer Maria Rilke

FOREWORD

I have written on the subject of faith before. In fact, I have taught courses on the theology of faith.

As I was finishing one course, a student came to me and asked: "Why didn't you share more of yourself in this course?" I thought for a long time about that remark.

I think I have supplied all that was missing in my previous attempts at faith. And I think I have shared "more of myself" in these pages. I hope you will like it, or at least take it in gentle hands.

John Powell, S.J.
Loyola University of Chicago
1998

The Question:

Have you ever wondered, as most of us have, if you really believe in God, religion, and the reality of the Church?

For many of us, when the question of faith surfaced at some crisis point in life, it was painful and disquieting, sometimes weighing heavily within the stomach like undigested food. We were tempted to find some diversion.

Maybe for you it came at a time when your back was against a wall, and you wondered about resorting to prayer. But the words of prayer seemed to stick in your throat, and your mind questioned whether prayer is something real or only a shallow superstition.

Or it may have been a Sunday morning, when the bells of the nearby Church were summoning the faithful to praise and petition God, and you turned over uneasily in your warm bed before going back to sleep.

Or when you were planning your marriage, and you found yourself trying to decide between a candle-lit Church and the offices of the local Justice of the Peace.

Or it could have been when someone you had known and loved "passed away," and the thought struck like thunder: What really happens after death?

"Do I really believe in God and an after-life?" You heard the question and it would not sleep.

Pressures and prejudice.

Prejudice is everywhere. There is no shining Camelot that banishes all prejudice or precludes psychological programming. Most human decisions are made in the glands, not by the brain. You know it. I know it.

Something honest in us wants to shed all prejudice, programming, brainwashing. We hate the umbilical cords that shackle us to our past, destroying freedom of choice. We do not want candles, incense and stained-glass windows, just because we have been "brought up" that way.

Religion and patriotism are special areas of suspicion. Both seem to promote "convenient" truths, the kind that prejudice plays upon, the kind that comforts us in need but controls our conduct. We are suspicious. We feel manipulated. We don't want to believe because someone else wants us to. That would be mere capitulation, an abdication of our intelligence.

But not all the tyrants that enslave us are outside us. The parasites of human insecurity have invaded all of us. They are like little termites of terror telling us that it is safer to believe, offering a blanket for Linus. God—if God is really there—is not an aspirin whatever else God may or may not be.

Prejudice has many forms. It may be that a more angry devil is raging in my guts: an old smoldering resentment for the superstitious saints that have tormented me with a sense of guilt.

Then there was Daddy, Mommy, an old maid, and sanctimonious clergy snarling sermons they didn't really believe. There was Sister Supernun who threatened to turn anyone into a pillar of salt if he/she dared to look back. There were the backwash biographies of saints who went to heaven and sinners who went to hell. It may be that I want to reject faith just so all of them will be wrong.

However, we can't let prejudice, based on experiences of annoyance, make our decisions, either way. There must be some middle ground of free air and open-mindedness between the pressures of indoctrination and the prejudice of the blind rebellion of emotional reaction.

A new look, an open mind, and honest choice.

The ultimate decision about faith cannot be the fate of a straw man, easy to set up or knock down, depending on the barometric reading of the present moment. We can't afford the dishonesty of setting up such a silly version of God and faith that even an amateur could do a clean assassination job. Nor do we want a pollyannish version, normally fed to children, that people in their right mind could not accept and find helpful.

Our childhood concept of God and faith was, if nothing else, a child's thoughts in a child's world. God was either a sugardaddy and a slavemaster, depending on whom one listened to. What we can't do is go on clutching to or clashing with an infantile version of God and faith. We have to challenge the accuracy and helpfulness of images of God developed in childhood.

We need, when the ache of the question of faith is upon us, an open mind, one that is willing to rethink, revise, rejudge.

16

We have learned this necessity of openness from our contact with other human beings. We refuse to categorize friends and acquaintances or imprison them in a once-and-for-all judgment, fixed and forever. Don't we owe the same courtesy to God? First impressions are often misleading, very often distorted and always incomplete.

Our ideas of God, faith and Church have been built upon a limited experience by a limited understanding. They may well have suffered from the pressures and prejudices we could not resist. Our conclusion may have been premature.

This book is meant to be a guide to a new look.

I write as a brother in the flesh of our human experience. My own faith has been battered by doubt, frozen in long winters, reborn in a thousand springtimes. I would like, in these pages, to share my thoughts, feelings and experiences with you, to tell you about the way I have gone and what I have found.

The way you go and the decisions you make, must, of course, be your own. What I have decided and what I have become as a result of my decisions is uniquely mine and uniquely me. What you decide and what you will become as a result of your decisions must be uniquely yours and you.

I would be untrue to myself and to you if I tried to become just another pressure, trying to coerce an act of faith. A coerced act of faith is really no act of faith at all.

Stepping out into faith or non-faith can be frightening, if for no other reason than that you will find yourself somehow strangely alone at the moment of choice.

As the great psychoanalyst, Erich Fromm, wrote in *The Art of Loving:*

> *If I am like everybody else, if I have no feelings or thoughts which make me different, if I conform in custom, dress, ideas to the pattern of the group, I am saved, saved from the frightening experience of aloneness.*

CHAPTER ONE

The Beginnings of Faith

The atheistic logic works this way.
God is supposed to be all good and all
powerful. But there is evil in the world.
Therefore, God isn't all good if God does
nothing about it; or God isn't all power-
ful if God can't do anything about it.

When any human being encounters the logic of atheism in the concrete circumstances of his or her life, the occasion will be upsetting. Here is a description of my own encounter with atheism.

In the 1940s I was preparing to leave for the Jesuit Novitiate to become a priest. I wanted to say "goodbye" and "thank you" to the man across the street. My family was relatively poor, and he was relatively rich. So over the years he had given the three children in my family many little gifts.

I told him that I was going away to college, and we chatted amicably about this. Then he learned the college I was going to was a Jesuit Novitiate. His face got red and he leaned forward. "Don't go. You'll be wasting your time and talent." Obviously, he was upset. I didn't understand. Then he thundered: "There is no God. You'll be pouring your life down a drain."

"There cannot be a God who presides over this world as long as there are wars." He then told me about his son, how he was accepted into medical school, and had already graduated when he was drafted into the army during World War II. The poor son had come home completely shattered by the savagery of war. His hair was gray and his hands shook. He was never able to practice medicine again. "There is no God," the father insisted, "as long as there are wars."

The father continued, "Look, I know the Scriptures as well as you do. I was trained in a church in which the Scriptures were everything. And I am telling you: There is no God."

I didn't know what to say. I did not want to leave my fatherly neighbor with an argument. So I said simply: "Thank you for your opinion. And thank you, too, for the footballs, the roller skates, the baseball bats, the kites, and everything else. I really am very grateful."

After bowing out of an argument, I returned home. I really don't recall thinking much about what he had said or its impact on me. I don't even remember telling my family "our neighbor is an atheist. He does not believe in God."

Later, what he had said and his reasons for saying it were to come back to me, but not that night.

I had been a bright light in the boxing team at school, and the coach was expecting me back to go on to pugilistic glory. But, in my senior year at school, my Jesuit counselor had warned me to give up boxing. "You'll be using your head for many years to come, and we don't want you to show up with a battered brain." The last thing he said to me, as I was going out the door, was: "And don't tell anyone about your intentions to become a priest."

I remember asking him "Why?" and he shocked me. He said, "Because we Jesuits may not accept you." It was the first time that this had occurred to me.

But I did pass all the examinations, and I was accepted.

But before I go on to finish my story, let me tell you about my first recollections of faith. Apparently, the seed was planted, as far back as my memory goes, by my mother.

My dear mother was a woman of great faith. My father was a convert to the faith. They had met at a classy shoe store in the downtown area of Chicago, where Mother sold lingerie and Dad sold shoes. They were eventually married and I was third (and last) of their children.

I remember that my mother spoke out her feelings, while Dad "kept his own counsel." I think now that God channeled the graces of faith through my mother to me.

Near the end of her life, she negotiated the stairs of our home on her knees. She was very much afraid of falling and breaking a hip. Once she told me that she was halfway down when she remembered that she had not said her "morning prayers." "So what did you do, Mom?" I asked naively. She looked at me almost indignantly, and said, "Naturally, I crawled back upstairs and said my prayers."

But no scene in my memory better portrays her sense of faith than her dying. She had a big picture of the Sacred Heart of Jesus at the foot of her bed. The day I confided to her that I was afraid of death, she leaned over to me and said: "I'm not afraid at all of dying. But I am afraid of pain. Looking at the picture of Jesus, she added, "So I said to the Lord: 'When you come for me, please tiptoe in here and kiss me while I am sleeping.'" Of course, she did die in her sleep, and I clearly remember saying to the picture of the Lord, which was still hanging at the foot of her deathbed, "You couldn't refuse her anything, could you?"

While she was dying, she was breathing unevenly. I remember straining forward to check that she had not in fact "breathed her last." I was holding her hand. I thought of all that hand had done for me. It was the hand that rubbed liniment on my chest when I had a cold, the had that placed cool cloths on my forehead when I was nauseous. But as I now reconstruct the scene, I feel the liniment and cool cloths had flowed naturally from her strong mother's instinct. The real gift—the lasting gift—was FAITH.

Just before she lost consciousness for the last time, I asked her if she would take care of us "when you get to heaven." Her weak reply was, "Yes, of course." I remember saying to her: "C'mon, Lady, say it like you mean it. Now once more with feeling." I can still see her as she filled her tired lungs with air. She bellowed: "Yes!" "Good. Now I heard you and so did everyone else in this place. You had better come through."

And so she has. It may sound a bit strange, but she has proved especially good at finding parking places. On a recent birthday, I entered a lot here at school that is always filled. I was sure that Jennie would not refuse me on my birthday. So I said a short prayer, and entered the lot. It was filled. So I had a little word with Jennie. "How could you? On the very day you gave birth to me?"

Just then a young woman entered the lot by foot and said: "I'm just leaving. You can have my place if you want it." Naturally, I apologized to the Queen.

. . . But let's go back now to the Novitiate.

CHAPTER TWO

The "Boot Camp" of Faith

No one believes 100 percent. Once upon a time, Lyndon Johnson, then president of the United States, tapped his foot on the floor, and announced that his faith was as firm as the floor. No doubt that he thought so. But in fact his faith was fragile, as it is with other human beings. Now, no doubt, he knows.

A bumper crop of novices entered the Society of Jesus in the '40s. Chuck Conroy and I entered from the same school, and entered the same day. When we went to our designated dormitory, we saw a tall, cassocked figure kneeling at his desk. His eyes were closed and his hands folded in prayer. Chuck and I were afraid he was asleep and would hurt himself. But we went to mark our clothes with an assigned laundry number, and when we returned to the dormitory, the cassocked figure was in the same position. Chuck and I were now sure that he was asleep, so we tapped him on the shoulder. We were astonished when he looked straight at us, as alert as can be, and said, "Yes." So we offered him some candy and he declined. And we went away.

We went to bed at 9 P.M. Unable to sleep, I remember looking at the dormitory ceiling and wondering if this was to be my life.

My first temptation, however, was not to leave. That would have been easier. My first temptation was against faith itself. Everything I had based my life on was somehow at stake. Someone has said that when more weight is put on faith, either the faith will buckle or grow stronger. Later when I read *The Screwtape Letters* by C.S. Lewis, in which the chief devil sends out his henchmen with specific instructions as to how each person is to be tempted, I thought of myself and faith. What if the man across the street at home was right? What if there is no God, as he said?

I reasoned within myself that, if this is God's boot camp, I can endure it. But what if there is no God? I could not think of a spookier way to spend my life. Yet I continued to march in the long black line with my fellow novices. One trouble was that most or many of the other novices did not seem to have my problem. They would shake their heads and whisper prayers in the chapel with great devotion. I wanted to tap one of them on the shoulder and ask: "Do you know something I do not? You seem to be getting through." But we were not allowed to do this. The only person with whom we could discuss such matters was the Master of Novices.

So I went to the Novices' Chapel and said quietly: "May-day. This is May-day. If you have something to say to me, say it now, and say it loud and clear. Otherwise, I'm pretty sure the ship is going down." Pause. Nothing.

So I went to the larger community chapel, somehow believing I could get better service, and said the same thing. The result was strikingly similar. Nothing. So I continued to march in the long back line, speaking Latin, praying three hours a day, and wondering if all this made any sense.

One night a moth tried to get through the screen to the light on my desk. Poor guy hit the screen, fell away and then tried again and again. I remember leaning over to tell him that I was going through the same experience. "They are screening me out too, fella."

I have since learned through the Enneagram of personality types that I am a worrier and a questioner. A friend who knows the Enneagram much better than I frequently asks me: "What are you asking and what are you worrying about today?" If I were the chief devil, this is where I would strike, if I really wanted to tempt myself. I would stir up questions in my mind and worries in my heart.

At any rate, sweaty hands and all, I finally went in to see the Master of Novices. I told him that I didn't believe any more. He nodded, "Be patient, Carissime" (*dearly beloved* in Latin). I thought he might send me back to Chicago, but he simply told me to be patient. "You're not listening, Father. I just told you that I think I am an atheist." He resumed his paternal manner, and reiterated his advice to "be patient."

Novices begin all prayer with "an act of presence." The Master of Novices had explained to us that God is always smiling down at us, though we raise our minds and hearts only infrequently. The act of presence is meant to achieve this contact with the smiling face of God. Needless to say, up to this point, I saw no one "smiling" or even looking down upon me.

Then one night, after four hours of "atheism," it happened. God touched me, during the act of presence. I stood by my desk, visibly shaken and sobbing. I remember the novice who had the desk behind mine standing in front of me. "Are you homesick?" he asked. The otherwise miserable novitiate was transformed into a heaven on earth. I couldn't wait to tell the Master of Novices.

"Guess what?" I began. He seemed to know, and we both recognized now the value of his "Be patient!" He took a book down from his shelf and told me to read the seventh chapter: "The Touch of God." It described my experience. The rest of the Novitiate was a snap.

I have described all this in a little booklet called *Touched by God*. (The same Master of Novices used to say if a thing is worth saying, it is worth repeating.) While this little book is by no means a best seller, it has brought to my desk more correspondence than anything I have ever written. Many of these letters tell me of a similar experience. I will mention some of them later.

The booklet was recently rewritten, and an epilogue was added. I wish now that I had some inkling of what was going on in me at that time. For now, let me say only this. I think self-knowledge is an absolute requisite for sanctity. Otherwise, people do not understand themselves well enough to detect their particular temptations and delusions. Likewise, one does not understand that one must be patient and await the hour of God. Many people, I feel, are just spinning their wheels.

You see (between you and me), I think that very few people really know themselves. They never arrive at self-understanding, and hide behind an image of what they think others would prefer. Most of us deal out a phony self. I think that self-observation is essential. I have taught young people, between the ages of eighteen and twenty-two, and for years have had my students write a faith-journal. I have read every page of these journals. Most of these young people underestimate themselves. They do not believe in their great potential. So they succumb to the pretense trap. Or they flail at themselves for repeatedly falling into the same faults.

Recently a medical doctor was in to see me. She said she was a "reader" at Mass, and certainly believed when she was performing this function. "Yet," she added, "when I go into the hospital to care for patients, I seemingly have no faith, except in the results of medical tests." Somehow it has almost been the same thing for me in teaching theology. In most of my classes there were students who did not believe, who believed in a different faith, some quite different. I tried not to impose on them my faith, even to the point of reading the Koran, the Talmud and Protestant authors. And this has led me to a weakening or questioning of my own faith.

I read Catholic authors, too, and heard many of them capsizing to the same doubts I had. One Catholic author said the first "hard fact" in the life of Jesus was his baptism at the Jordan. All that precedes this is not to be trusted. Another Catholic author said that if the remains of Jesus were dug up in Jerusalem, it would not disturb his faith at all. Apparently, he did not consider the physical resurrection of Jesus to be essential. Some of the leading Catholic Scripture scholars were of little consolation.

When I read the Scriptures I read of Jesus curing and healing, and I wonder why such healings are not more common in the Church today. My doubts even extended to myself. I have a long history of "daily Communion." I used to think of this daily Communion during my school years as preserving me from the normal temptations of adolescence. The men with whom I live in community also have a long history of daily Mass and

Communion. Why aren't we all more angelic? Why are we so like others? Why am I so like others? Why doesn't daily Communion make more of a difference?

When I was teaching in a seminary, the dean of the theologate assigned me to be the moderator of a cinema workshop. When I protested that I knew nothing of movie making, he assured me that my function was only to referee discussions. Anyway, the rhythm of the seminar was this. We saw a movie, then we discussed it, and finally saw it again. One such movie was *Agnes of God.* It seemed that all the Nuns in this medieval convent were possessed by the devil, except one. The untroubled one, the gatekeeper, had constructed a tunnel to the local pub, where she quaffed one with the boys and played the guitar. When they asked her why the devil left her alone, she responded: "I just don't know."

The author of the book on which the movie was based was intrigued by the question of the repression of human nature. Flashed on the screen at the beginning were his doubts. Were the Sisters really possessed by the devil, or had they repressed nature so much that this resulted in their strange "possession?" My mind traveled back to the Novitiate and my own experiences of the interventions of God. Had it all been a delusion? Or had I really experienced the power, presence and peace of God? The questioner, the doubter and the worrier were suddenly alive and well within me.

CHAPTER THREE

The Experience of Faith

Most of the things we know are known by experience. The taste of chocolate ice cream, a day in the Autumn of the year, the sting of a bee. In fact, love itself is a matter of experience. Some psychiatrists deny the very existence of love. They say it is a delusion. But when one has either loved or been loved, it is all clear. Love exists. But we can know this only by experience.

In the movie, *A Patch of Blue,* the blind girl asks her grandfather: "Old paw, what's green like?" The irritated old man answers: "Green is green, Stupid. Now stop asking questions." There follows a pathetic scene in which the young girl paws the grass with her hand and rubs a leaf against her cheek. She is vainly trying to experience the reality of greenness.

The playwright, William Alfred, author of *Hogan's Goat,* once said: "People who tell me that there is no God are like a six-year-old saying that there is no such thing as passionate love. They just haven't experienced God yet."

Recently I heard by mail from a Scottish person. His marriage was on the rocks. Things were in a definite nosedive pattern. He wrote that, when he was outside, and no one could hear him, he screamed to God: "There has to be something better than this!" No sooner than the words were spoken, a definite feeling of joy entered him. The joy was soon almost ecstasy. He is now a teacher at his church, a reader at Mass, and a happily married man.

At the same time I heard from an Irish Doctor, who told me of attending a Mass at Harbu Camp in Ethiopia in 1985. Three different nurses invited him to a Mass. Finally, "I dragged myself off my bed, cursing the good intentions of my nurse friends, and the conscience which my Catholic upbringing had saddled me with."

His letter continued: "Without undue excitement, I became aware that I was in the presence of a warm, personal, comforting Jesus Christ. This presence seemed to fill and enrich the atmosphere in that bedraggled, humble room. . . . I became aware that almost unknown to me my entire being had become filled with a warmth, comfort and contentment, which I had never experienced before. The knowledge of this presence was almost blinding in its intensity. . . . I thought consciously that I had done nothing to merit this gift. My overall impression was a sense of great generosity coming from a source way beyond me."

Then there was Bill Wilson. He was one of the two founders of the Alcoholics Anonymous movement. He was a chronic alcoholic and his doctor, Wm. D. Silkworth, M.D., patiently and repeatedly dried him out. Bill had been the darling of Wall Street until he descended into a liquor-soaked despair. Dr. Silkworth finally decided to confront Bill with the facts: "You are a chronic alcoholic. There is nothing more I can do for your except to take your money, and I don't want to do that."

A former drinking partner, Ebby T., had once tried to get Bill interested in prayer and religion. "Ebby, what on earth has got into you? What is this all about?" Ebby simply replied: "I've got religion." Bill later said of Ebby: "Then, very dangerously, he touched on the subject of prayer and God. He frankly said he expected me to balk at these notions." But Ebby went on to say that ever since he attempted prayer, the results he experienced had been immediate. Not only had he been released from his desire to drink, he had also found peace of mind and happiness of a kind he had not known for years. However, at that earlier time all Ebby's efforts with Bill were unsuccessful.

Once again, back at Towns Hospital where Bill had recently been dried out with barbiturates and bella donna, suicidal Bill Wilson cried out: "I'll do anything, anything at all! If there is a God let Him show Himself."

I quote now from the book *Pass It On,* (a biography of Bill Wilson) p. 121.

> *What happened next was electric. Suddenly, my room*
> *blazed with an indescribably white light. I was seized*

with an ecstasy beyond description. Every joy I had known was pale by comparison. The light, the ecstasy—I was conscious of nothing else for a time. . . . Then came the blazing thought: You are a free man.

The book continues: "Bill Wilson said that after that experience, he never again doubted the existence of God, and he never took another drink."

I am reminded of what I once told my students in class. I used to tell them that God is like an electrical outlet. You can light a room, wash the dishes, show a movie, etc., but you have to get plugged in. And the plug-in is faith.

In my favorite miracle passage in the New Testament, Jesus is walking along with his disciples. Everyone is pushing and shoving Him. Then suddenly He straightens up, and announces to his astonished disciples: "Someone just touched me with a touch of faith." "So how did you know that?" the bewildered Apostles asked. He answered: "I felt my healing power go out of me."

Jesus looked down at the side of the road, and there was a little woman. She admitted that the touch was hers. She told him the story of how she had been afflicted with hemorrhages for years, how she had spent all of her money on doctors, and how she knew that if she could just touch the hem of his garment she would be cured. Like Bill Wilson, twenty centuries later, she was desperate. (See *Mark,* 5:24–35)

I keep wondering if the condition of desperation might well release us to the power of God. I keep wondering if, when we finally decide we are nothing, and cannot make it on our own, God decides to give us the grace that will enable us to make something of ourselves. Maybe some of us have to be desperate.

Leonard Cohen once wrote a song called *Suzanne.* In it he says:

> *And Jesus was a sailor*
> *when He walked upon the water;*
> *only drowning men could see Him.*

But Jesus could be a ghost, a delusion. Maybe we have been brainwashed. Maybe the gospels are fiction. Freud claims, in his book *The Future of an Illusion,* that faith is an invention of the unconscious mind. Freud contends: God did not create us. We created God.

I often wonder why people flock to weeping icons and bleeding statues. Why the devotion to Padre Pio who seemed to know everything? Why do the faithful flock to Medugorje? I suspect that some of them are seeking some experiential confirmation of their faith.

I remember the tour I took of the Holy Land. I roomed with another priest who snored very loudly. At the end of the tour we docked at Bari, Italy. I looked at the itinerary back to Rome, where we were both studying. I saw that our train passed through Foggia, and I recognized it as the district of Padre Pio. I soon conned the priest who was with me to stop off there. He agreed that he "owed me one," because of the snoring, so we stopped off to see the "mobile shrine of Lourdes." When we arrived, a little Capuchin Brother told us that we could not see Padre Pio. However, he did arrange a meeting with Padre Eustachio (Fr. Eustace) who handled Padre Pio's correspondence in English.

Padre Eustachio did concede that Padre Pio seemed to know everything, though he cautioned us not to "sniff around for miracles." He told us of the time he was about to say Mass, and noticed that the date was the fifth anniversary of his father's death back in England. He also noticed that Padre Pio was about to say Mass. So he went to him, with the intention of asking prayers for his father. "Excuse me, Padre Pio," was all he could say before Padre Pio turned to him and said. "I have already prayed for your father."

I had to ask Fr. Eustace about one "miracle," of which I had read. Padre Pio had promised the people in his town, San Giovanni Rotundo, that they would never be bombed during the war. However, an English pilot was about to bomb San Giovanni Rotundo in Foggia, and was the leader of his squadron. Suddenly the pilot who was an atheist saw a super life-sized priest with arms extended, in the sky. He thought he was cracking up, but radioed to his squadron, and they all veered off.

Padre Eustachio confirmed that this was authentic. The pilot later saw a picture of Padre Pio in a magazine. and asked: "Who is this priest?" The pilot later converted "to the faith" and "comes every year to make a retreat under Padre Pio." Then there was a sudden knock on the door. It was the Brother who greeted us and told us we could not see Padre Pio. His announcement was that Padre Pio was in the corridor, and that we could see him there.

We greeted the saintly Padre Pio, and he told us jokes for about fifteen minutes. My priest friend was very impressed. I was slightly disappointed. I have asked myself about that meeting innumerable times. I guess I expected Padre Pio to say something mysterious and prophetic. I suppose I wanted my faith confirmed. I wanted to hear some extraordinary revelation of Padre Pio's knowledge.

CHAPTER FOUR

The Credibility of Faith

When St. Paul tells the Romans (12:1) that faith is a reasonable submission which we make to God, he is talking about the credibility (the believability) of faith. Faith and human reason are not opposed to each other. Faith remains a "blind leap," but it is not an "irrational leap," a leap which is contrary to reason. In fact, there are circumstances which point to the probability of the truth obtained by faith.

Caryll Houselander was an English author. One of the books she wrote was called *A Rocking Horse Catholic*. Presumably, the book got its title from the fact that Caryll was baptized into the faith at the age when little girls in England play on rocking horses.

At one stage of her conversion she asked her uncle, called "Old Smokey," because of the pipe he smoked: "Do you believe in the New Testament?" The elderly uncle, who was an attorney at law, drew deeply upon his pipe and then answered the precocious child: "Why yes, I do.

"I do because, being an attorney, I know guilty parties always have an alibi, carefully put together. They always know where they were when the crime was being committed. They were somewhere else (*alibi,* in Latin). The New Testament wasn't written until Jesus had been dead more than thirty years. If its authors had intended to lie, they could have done a much better job. After all, they had thirty years to prepare. They would not have put in some of the apparent contradictions they did include. They would not have Jesus proclaiming that he was the Son of God and then on the cross crying out: 'My God, my God, why have you forsaken me?'"

"Old Smokey" was seemingly saying that the New Testament was not a lie. The Apostles who were near to Jesus during his life on this earth all (with the exception of St. John) died martyrs. They would not have died for a lie.

Also, if they were in the process of making up a religion, they should have made up an easier one. The commandment to "love your enemies," would have to go. They should have been more lenient in the matter of chastity. And they could have been better at explaining away suffering than: "Let the person who wants to follow me, take up his cross and follow me." They should have invented a simpler and more painless religion.

It is almost inconceivable that Jesus could have started a movement as widespread and lasting as Christianity, with the "boneheads" he chose. Peter always had footprints around his mouth, and Jimmy and Johnny were "Mama's Boys." Thomas is said to be a twin, but the twin never shows up. So the early Christian writers argued that Thomas was half-saint and half-bullhead. Philip was the soul of sincerity but a little naive. And these were among the best.

But all these arguments are arguments for the credibility or believability of faith. They do not persuade one to take the "blind leap" into faith. Still, the odds against Christianity starting this way would seem to predict it would result in a colossal failure.

To say that Christianity is an improbable success story is almost like saying that the way a dictionary was first printed was when a print shop blew up, and all the letters came down in the form of the dictionary. Or finding a watch in a desert, and saying the parts just fell off of some tree and came together. It just doesn't seem logical.

Hardly.

CHAPTER FIVE

Faith: What It Isn't

A professional baseball player, who enjoyed playing only on grass, said: "If cows can't eat it, I don't want to play on it." It is a truism of faith that, "if you can reason to it, it isn't faith."

As I mentioned earlier, I taught theology to students for thirty years. When I asked them if they believed, a great majority would say they did. It was when I got around to asking them why they believed that I got a variety of answers.

Some said: "I'm Italian . . . I'm Irish . . . I'm Spanish . . . I'm African American." It was almost as though faith ran along blood lines. I suggested that this was not true faith.

Others thought that faith was a good hunch. If you believe, you don't have to put in a great deal of effort, and if there is a God, you're saved. If not, it is not a great deal of wasted effort. The late George Jessel, an after-dinner speaker, said he talked at Catholic, Protestant, and Jewish dinners, because "it doesn't hurt to hedge your bets." This attitude of openness to all beliefs was easy to demolish as true faith.

The third set of answers, which I think a majority of students held, was that reason can find God. This, strangely enough, is true. Thomas Aquinas thought that there were five ways in which reason can lead us to the existence of God. The simplest is his theory of causality. For every effect there is a proportionate cause. If I see a billiard ball move, I know that something moved it. To explain the effect of this complicated world there also has be a proportionate cause. An uncaused cause. True, but not faith. Aquinas felt that there were very few minds which could follow his logic, but insisted that faith is never the conclusion of a line of logic.

John Cardinal Newman, in one way or another, is forever stressing the same thing. Faith is not the result of a natural, logical process. It is precisely *not* a conclusion from premises. In the next chapter, we will be talking about what faith *is*. For now it is enough to say that faith is not an acquisition of the natural mind alone.

For this reason if you find two people debating the reality of faith, the only conclusion one can come to is that they are both "lightweights." Faith can never be proved or disproved.

I remember, when I was in high school, walking one night with a classmate. The moon was swimming through the clouds, and it was a very beautiful sight. My friend remarked, "It is difficult to see how there could be an atheist." I was impressed at the time. But faith remains an acceptance of God's word to us. I can reason that there is an "uncaused cause" but the fact that God has spoken to us, that God cares about us, remains in the realm of faith.

Once I was sitting in the room of a fellow Jesuit priest. I noticed trees were painted on his walls, and inquired about the artist. "Oh, I did that," he responded factually. "You see, I had a near-death experience, and after that I have been afraid of nothing. I thought that if I made a mess of this, I could splash more paint on the walls, or paper them." When I inquired about his near-death experience, he told me of his open-heart surgery.

"While I was under the anesthetic, I was in a room with a man, who never identified himself as Jesus, but who knew everything about me. He kept a consoling hand on my shoulder, assuring me that we were not ready for the 'big trip' yet. The poor doctors could not get my heart beating again after they had replaced it, and were trying everything: electrical stimulation, massage, and so forth. When I finally emerged from the anesthetic, I felt very calm. The poor doctors were standing around me sweating profusely. 'We thought we had lost you,' they said. By contrast I felt very confident and calm."

When a girl was attacked and killed on her way to this university, my priest-friend said he was standing alone on a platform with a microphone. It was his job as a University Minister to calm down the students. Later, a young man known for his holiness, asked the priest: "Who was that man standing at your side tonight?" The priest demurred, "There was no one at my side tonight. I was alone." "Oh, Father, c'mon. He had his hand on your shoulder." The priest then asked, "What did he look like?" The young man described the person who had been in the room with the priest during his open-heart surgery.

When Dr. Elizabeth Kubler-Ross heard of this, she advised the priest to tell his story to the world. "It is very important, you know." Dr. Kubler-Ross thinks that this is not an age of faith, and that people today will not believe unless preternatural events are proved to them. Near-death experiences are one way to help some persons acknowledge God's existence. It may be that near-death experiences can prove to people that there is an afterlife, but still this is not faith. Anything that can be proved is not faith.

CHAPTER SIX

Faith: What It Is

Then Simon Peter spoke up: "You are the Messiah, the Son of the living God." "Good for you, Simon, son of John!" answered Jesus. "Because this truth did not come to you from any human being or from your own human resources. It was given to you directly by my father in heaven."

$\mathcal{F}$aith is a pure gift of God. I say "pure gift" because every attraction to faith and faith itself must be the result of God's action in us.

I used to ask my students: "Can God put an idea, a conviction in our minds?" If God can put an idea or conviction in the human mind, then indeed faith is a "reasonable submission" to the action of God. On the other hand, if God cannot do this, I see no reason for calling this submission "faith."

But first let me try to distinguish between mind and will. These are the two highest faculties or powers of human beings. It is these two faculties that distinguish us from brute beasts. The mind or intellect is the power by which we know. The three powers of the mind are 1) getting ideas 2) putting together or separating ideas: judging 3) linking one idea to another: reasoning.

The will is the faculty in us which chooses, is attracted to something or someone, which is perceived as "a good." As far as we know the will is a blind faculty. The mind perceives the alternatives of a choice, and the will is attracted to the "goods" proposed to it. If its choice involves a moral good or bad, it is said to be a moral choice. For example, I find your wallet. It contains much money. Now immediately I know through my mind that I can give it back to you or keep it. My mind presents the benefits of each alternative to my will. My power of choice (my will) attracts me to give back your wallet or to keep it.

I may choose to return your wallet. But if I choose to keep it, the will thrusts back on the mind the onus or burden of rationalizing my choice. The mind then proceeds to justify the choice. "After all, it was good old Robin Hood who stole from the rich and gave to the poor. I am only doing what Robin Hood did."

In the matter of faith, the process just described here is reversed. In this case, the first grace of God is extended to the will. I am attracted to believe. How? It depends on my personal inclinations. I may be attracted to God as the source of order or beauty. I may be attracted to God in other people, or the love of others. There are many ways to be attracted to God.

The second and more decisive grace is given to the mind which makes the act or judgment of faith. The God to whom I am attracted gives my mind the power to believe. God says to the human being: It is true that I care for you; it is true that I have a destiny for you in my house. It is true that I have spoken to you through the patriarchs, prophets and psalmists of the Old Testament. And it is true that I have spoken to you though my Son. When a human being answers this call of God by saying, "I believe" it is the blind leap, or as the philosopher Kierkegaard once put it: "the absolute paradox." It is the discovery of the pearl of great price.

Ordinarily, when we assent to a truth, we demand proof first, and then we are convinced. In faith, we believe because God, who cannot be deceived and will not deceive us, has enabled us first and simply to believe whatever God says or has said. Then we proceed to try to understand what God has said. In fact, St. Anselm of Canterbury defined theology as "faith in search of understanding." I believe so that I might understand. In my own trials and tribulations of faith, I have looked for a comparison. Is there a human experience in which faith and commitment precede understanding?

I think that one comparison is the faith that husband and wife have at the moment of their vowed commitment. If the woman were to ask the man, "Will you be a good husband?" he could only reply, "I'll try." She has to believe this. She has to believe in him. And vice versa. Their commitment to each other will take them to places they do not dream of at the moment of their vows. It is like getting into a boat for a voyage over uncharted waters.

Marriage and faith in God are similar in this respect. Both demand commitment at the beginning before proof is available. Faith has also been compared to a stained glass window. From the outside the beauty is not available. From the inside, with the sun streaming through the window, the beauty is undeniable. So it is with faith. When one stands only on the outside of faith, the peace and power of believing is not available. *On the inside of faith, the presence and peace of God come streaming through.*

Faith has also been compared to a new pair of glasses. Through the eyes of faith, everything looks different. One sees the value of everything more clearly through the eyes of faith. While others scratch and claw for the things of this world, the believer is largely spared this competition. The believers know that it profits persons nothing to gain the whole world, but suffer the loss of their own souls.

So how do things look different? For one thing the motive of a believer is love. And the love is reserved in the believer for other human beings. The late Mother Teresa is a good example of this. She said quite openly that the face of Jesus was visible in the faces of the needy and homeless. And obviously if things look different, the choice of things will be different. Consequently the motivation of the believer, the reason why we choose this or that, is different from non-believers.

At the beginning of Chapter Two, we said that no one believes 100 percent. I have a congenital disease of the eyes called *retinitis pigmentosa.* I was in my twenties when the disease, which is inherited through the genes, was first diagnosed. The poor ophthalmologist looked very sad as he informed me that "someday you may well be blind." I have since had his diagnosis confirmed by other eye doctors. I used to say, as my eyes remained unchanged, "if God wants my eyesight," I have told God: "take it, it's yours."

But now, as God does seem actually to be taking it, my reaction is quite different. I am now legally blind. If I step back far enough from my emotional reaction, the whole situation becomes very interesting from the standpoint of faith. It is something like "putting your money where your mouth is." As my eyesight grows weaker, I hear distinct echoes of "take it, it's yours." Everyone has a similar situation. The question which the situation asks deep within a person is this: Do you really believe? How deeply do you believe? No one believes a hundred percent. I realize now how fragile my faith offering was in my twenties. Somehow I feel more real about faith now.

I suppose all suffering poses these questions. Suffering is a gift which no one wants. Very few of the saints among us ask for suffering. Yet when it comes into our lives, we do ask questions which we had never asked before. It is possible to think that because we have faith this God-given knowledge answers all questions. But this does not seem true in the extremes of pain and suffering. In actuality, we grow in faith to meet these new challenges. I suppose that this is one of God's reasons for allowing us to suffer: we grow in faith. We trust that the goodness and love of God for us are operating for our benefit, precisely through our suffering.

In other words, God is asking through suffering: How much, how deeply, do you really believe? The ultimate challenge to faith, of course, is death. When death comes to each of us, as indeed it will, we will be asked: "Do you really believe? Do you really believe in an after-life, that I have a destiny for you? Do you really believe that I love you?"

I recall driving an elderly priest (now deceased) in my community to see his family. Believing as I do that the only time you really get to know a person is when you share what is deepest,

I asked him, "Do you think we really believe? I have rarely seen anyone jump for joy at the announcement of death." He paused for a moment and then reflected, "The will to live is the strongest instinct in us. There are many other instincts in us, but by far the instinct to live is the most powerful. As one gets older, of course, death becomes more congenial. But all the old instincts still live on in us. Besides, everyone has some fear in change. Death is a permanent change, leaving behind everything that we have known. The passage into eternity is made just once."

Then there are those who take a different view of death.

I was reminded of the young man in class, who professed that he wasn't afraid of death. I remember he said that "It will be interesting to see what happens. Naturally, I don't want to die yet. I want a profession and a family in this life. But when my time comes it will be oh so interesting to see what God has in store for us."

A psychologist once wrote a dissertation about whether faith was a comfort in the moment of death. His conclusion was that faith is a comfort when it has been integrated into daily living, but faith is not a comfort when it is a matter of pious celebrations of

Easter, Christmas, and so forth. God does not wait well in the wings of the stage of life. If a person has to think a long time to remember the last thing he or she did because they believe, faith probably has not been integrated into life. It is a matter of the old question: "If you were tried for being a Christian, would there be enough evidence to convict you?"

Of course, there is much about what is accepted by faith that I do not fully understand. I remember meeting a woman who once said to me: "You know, when I die and meet God, what I want to ask Him?" Naturally, I said: "No, what do you want to ask God?" Her answer was: "Everything." Today our culture demands independence of us. We are supposed to be able to deal with anything. We're supposed to have everything "under control." And yet faith asks submission of us in matters we do not fully understand.

A famous psychiatrist of our day once said that the three parts of love are: kindness, encouragement and challenge. *Kindness* tells the beloved: "I am with you. I am on your side. I am in your corner. Whatever I do or say is an act of love." *Encouragement* means giving the beloved courage in him or herself. A common temptation is doing for others what they can do for themselves.

There is always the danger of what is called "co-dependency." The true lover says: "Believe in yourself, in the gifts that have already been given to you." The third part of love is *challenge:* "Find a way to do it! Just do it."

God seems to love us in all these ways. In the beginning of my life, I sat in God's lap. God was very kind to me. God told me in indelible language that I was loved. I knew then I could accept myself as I was. Then God encouraged me to believe in myself, in the gifts that had already been given to me. When things go wrong or at least as I had not planned them I think God is testing me. God is then challenging me.

Quite naturally, there is much I do not understand about faith. It remains the "blind leap," the "absolute paradox." I believe that God is attracting me to a deeper and more trusting faith. Things look quite different when they are transformed by looking through the eyes of faith. I recall what the late Secretary General of the United Nations, Dag Hammarskjold, once wrote: "On the day I first believed, the world made sense to me, and life had a new meaning for me."

CHAPTER SEVEN

Faith and Religious Experience

Pierre Teilhard de Chardin, a man of extraordinary intelligence, writes in The Divine Milieu: "I see and touch God everywhere. Everything means both everything and nothing to me. Everything is God to me; everything is dust to me. Yes, Lord God, I believe. . . . It is not just your gifts that I discern; it is You yourself that I encounter, you who cause me to share in your being, and whose hands mold me."

*A*ll relationships thrive on communication. The relationship with God in faith is no exception. How we speak to God is clear to most people. We say prayers to God. We ask for things. We praise

God for the apparent goodness and lavishness of creation. But how does God speak back to us? For most of us this remains a mystery. We wait to see how things turn out. Then, like the lepers who were cleansed in the gospel-stories, most of us never go back to say "thank you."

In fact, I am rather "big" on gratitude. I used to write about five-hundred letters every year recommending this or that student for acceptance into graduate school, law school, medical school, and so forth. About one out of every ten students would return to say: "I got accepted! Thank you for the letter." When only one of the lepers came back, Jesus asked him: "Where are the other nine? There were ten, were there not?" Whenever I pray about this scene I tell Jesus he is running about average. The gifts which come to us are from the generosity of God, not as a result of our demands. The hands of God open to us more easily when we are grateful. All is gift. Through gratitude we become more conscious of God's loving presence in our lives. Strictly speaking, we don't have a right to religious experience.

There is a story I once heard which seems to describe "religious experience" very well. It is a story of a small boy, flying a kite. The kite is surrounded and hidden by a low-flying cloud. A man comes along and says to the boy who is flying the kite, "Hey Kid, what are you doing with that string in your hand?" The boy replies, "I'm flying my kite." The man looks up and says, "I don't see a kite up there." And the boy responds, "I don't either, but I know that there is a kite up there. I feel tugs on the kite string."

For me this story describes well how God speaks back to us: "Tugs on the kite string." An agnostic can easily pass us by and say, "I don't see a God up there." But we can remain sure, simply because of "tugs on the kite string."

I remember a young woman who had to withdraw from the university where I was teaching. Her mother had developed Alzheimer's disease, and so she withdrew to nurse her mother through this long goodbye. Two years later she came in to see me. She told me that her mother had died. She said that, "With Alzheimer's you never know when people are going to die. However, before my mother died I went to a bank. As I was waiting in line, an enormous peace came over me. I looked at the clock on the bank wall. A quarter to two. The time seemed meaningless. I transacted what I came to do and left the bank. When I returned home, the paramedics were outside my house. I could see the flashing lights on their vehicle. When I entered my house, they suggested I sit down, and told me my mother had died. "At what time?" I asked. Then they told me, "A quarter to two."

Tugs on the kite string.

Another very helpful recollection. When I was in high school, my mother came home from the school where she taught with the news that "Helen Bradley is dying." Helen Bradley was also a teacher. So as a family we said a short prayer for Helen Bradley. Then several months later, Mother came home from school with the news that Helen Bradley had been "cured."

It seems that Helen had terminal cancer. She had written to Padre Pio, the Italian Capuchin priest, known for his holiness, and had asked for his prayers for her recovery. One night as she was sitting with her sister she detected a strong aroma of roses. She asked her sister if she had perhaps spilled some perfume. The sister replied: "It's the cancer. Now it has affected your sense of smell." When a friend came to see her later that evening, Helen asked if the guest detected an aroma of roses. When the friend did not, Helen exclaimed, "I think I've been cured."

Helen returned to the Catholic hospital at which she had had two operations. The doctor was a bit impatient. He told her to go home, say her prayers, and prepare to die. So Helen demanded another examination. The doctor reluctantly gave her another exam, and was quite surprised. There was no trace of the cancer. Helen asked him to testify that this had indeed been a miracle. The doctor replied: "Helen, I have tried to keep this from you as long as possible. I do not believe in God. I will testify that you previously had a normally terminal cancer. On this later date, I can find no cancer at all. I don't know how this happened, but I'm not going to postulate a God just because of this. Perhaps it is spontaneous remission or something. I just don't know."

When, as a newly ordained priest, I said my first solemn high Mass in Chicago, a woman approached me for my blessing. Since I didn't recognize her, I asked about her identity, and she started to cry. "I'm Helen Bradley. God was good to me." I remember telling this story in class, only to have a student say he did not believe that story. "Why would God cure this one person and not everyone who has terminal cancer?" he asked. Either Helen Bradley had enough faith or God cured her to provide us with evidence for faith.

I say: "More tugs on the kite string." However, I am indebted to Helen Bradley for more than this. For the first time I understood why Jesus didn't do his works of power when there was no faith in this or that locale. It takes faith to recognize a miracle, the power of God. Otherwise, it's just "spontaneous remission" or something like that.

I have already mentioned my own mother and her dying promise "to take care of us" when she got to heaven. I am a strong believer in the communion of saints, that the living and the dead can communicate. I have talked out many different matters with my mother since her death. Her responses are among the tugs of my own kite string.

There is growing evidence that there is life after life. And—this will surprise you as it did me—over half the people in this country insist that they have had some contact with the deceased. And not a few medical doctors have assured us that patients who are prayerful or being prayed for do much better that those who are prayerless. One of the things that impressed me was that some of those who were being prayed for did not know of this. Still they did better.

Most of us know some "religious" people who are withered and angry. They rain down fire and brimstone on all those about them in the name of faith. There is no doubt that a neurotic religious experience has to be distinguished from an authentic experience of the power of God. Some of these phony religious experiences produce only disgust in us.

There must be some criteria for distinguishing the purely imagined from the authentic. I would suggest that there are three tests which should be applied. The first is the TIME test. Sometimes people in a moment of overcharged emotions report that they have felt the touch of God. If such an experience is in reality only a natural force of emotion, it will soon be spent and all effects will quickly disappear. However, if God has really entered our lives, we can never be the same again.

Secondly, there is the REALITY test. Delusory religious experience, invented to answer some subconscious need, such as feeling important or even the need to be punished, tends to isolate a person from reality. However, when God enters a life there is a deeper contact with reality. The recipients of such experiences will seem to be *more* alive, *more* aware of others and the world about them. Their perception of beauty will be keener and their compassion for the suffering ones among us will be greater.

Finally, there is the CHARITY test. When God truly enters a human life the result will be that those whom God touches will be more loving. Religious experience which produces self-complacency and self-righteousness cannot be from God. God is love, and he who abides in love abides in God.

True religious experience makes possible things like this: When we remain silent despite the urge to defend ourselves. . . . When we offer only justice and love to those who have treated us unfairly. . . . When we have completely forgiven another especially if we gain nothing from it. . . . When we have made an act of sacrifice without receiving any gratitude or acknowledgment. . . . When we have acted out of conscience, even though it seemed nonsensical. . . . When we give to another without the expectation of gratitude or even a sense that we have done the right thing. And so forth. These are genuine religious experiences. These are signs that God has been at work in us.

When believers start looking for God intently, we can begin to find God in all things. Chardin wrote in *The Divine Milieu:* "I see and touch God everywhere. Everything is God to me; everything is dust to me." There is a haunting possibility that I have not heard the voice of God because I have been too preoccupied with my own questions. I have been too busy speaking, to listen. Maybe we should pray with the Psalmist: "Create in me, O God, a loving and a listening heart!"

CHAPTER EIGHT

The Crises of Faith

One of my favorite ploys as a teacher was to come into a classroom and write two Chinese characters on the board. One says in Chinese: danger. The other says: opportunity. Together, in Chinese, they spell crisis. A crisis obviously can be a danger, but it can also be an opportunity.

There are seemingly three possible reactions to a crisis. The first is to deny that a given situation constitutes a crisis. This is possible in crises of daily life as well as in the crises of faith. The second possible reaction is to sweep the crisis under the rug. You admit that there is a crisis but refuse to face it. The third possibility is to talk or pray through the crisis.

I know from experience that, if a crisis of faith is survived, the faith of that person will forever be deeper. It is something like a broken bone. If the break is given a chance to heal, nature will throw out extra calcium around the break to make it stronger, and to insure that there will never be a break in that place again.

Crises of faith are inevitable. One of the accusations made against faith is that it is "brainwashing." It is true that in our earliest years we are simply rubber stamps of whatever our parents believe. But through personal experience of values and opinions we come to develop our own opinions, often very different from the opinions of our parents. Witness the preference in music of each new young generation. In childhood the most important developmental issue to be dealt with is selfishness. An understandable self-centeredness is the hallmark of childhood. Somewhere around the ages of nine to twelve, a sense of caring for others will start to become a reality to the child.

The faith-crisis in adolescence is related to one's sense of self-acceptance. In early adolescence, the young are distracted from the invitation to live by faith by a strong emotional appeal to break away from their parents. At this age the peer group is so important. The young adolescent tends to conform to the values important to the group. Middle adolescence covers the fifteenth to the eighteenth year. The experience in these years is the tension felt between the gregarious instinct and the instinct for individuation. The mid-adolescent wants to be a member of the group, but at the same time, wants to do his or her own thing. The great crisis of adolescence overall involves the development of self-acceptance, even though we are creatures of ambiguity. This is the discovery and challenge of the adolescent. What adolescents need is someone to understand and accept them on this journey with all their ambivalence, in spite of all their zigs and zags.

The most definitive time for faith-development among young people comes between the ages of eighteen and twenty-five. It has been called the "age of conversion." A part of these challenging years has been called the "age between homes." It is the age between the parental home and the home we hope for of our own. The college experience is above all a course in criticism. In English, in Science, and so forth, students are trained to question presuppositions. They are encouraged to work through trial and error. Even the theology of memorized statements has to be replaced by a theology of questioning. It is indeed a risky but necessary business. The young are taught to relinquish the security of previous opinions, and to accept the challenge of developing their own outlook on life.

Faith in adulthood is challenged by a crisis of meaning. The crisis of being over thirty is the crisis of boredom and repetition. Viktor Frankl suggests that the bread of life is "meaning." The crisis of being over thirty is the crisis of finding meaning in life. It is a time when we are too old to be young and too young to be old. Carl Jung, the great psychiatrist, once observed that most of his patients in middle life could find no "sense in living."

Jung writes:

> *They are depressed. They may ask themselves, "What next?" "Where am I going?" . . . Religious experience is missing in the lives of many people today. I am now convinced that I never had a case in middle life that did not originate in a spiritual unrest.*

In the matter of faith, we learn to question authorities until we have our own experiences and learn to think for ourselves. We have our own personal difficulties, and eventually by approaching these with faith, we mature into a faith of our own. Of course, this supposes a reasonable sincerity on the part of the seeker, and the gift of faith on the part of God. Paul Tillich once said that only through crises can faith mature. "Doubt must eat away the old form of faith so that a new and deeper faith can be born in us."

A noted preacher of our day was once asked, "How long does it take you to prepare one of your sermons?" The preacher replied: "All my life." Our yesterdays lie heavily upon our todays and our todays upon our tomorrows. All of our lives we are being shaped and we are shaping ourselves by past experiences. Mature faith depends largely on the following three discoveries which we make early in life.

I am told that the first discovery important to our development of faith is *otherness.* As infants, at approximately six months, we discovered at least vaguely that we were not the only existent beings. We were not even the center of our own worlds. It is obvious that our faith can only be as sound as is our acceptance of otherness. And we know that the process of mastering otherness has various degrees of success. We discover otherness only partially as infants.

The second discovery of infancy is *language.* Sometime during the second year of life, formerly unintelligible sounds begin to sound like words, and words fall into sentences. Language is obviously a gift to help us achieve the communication of ourselves. It can also be used manipulatively. Whatever limitations we suffer in this matter will condition the authenticity of our faith. The world of religion and faith is filled with words. If we mean them we will eventually arrive at a true faith. If we do not mean them, but use them manipulatively, we will arrive only at pretense.

The third discovery made at about the age of five is *conscience.* We are challenged by this important developmental step which leads us from coercive regulation of conduct to personal behavior based on internalized values. The formation of conscience is subject to the same possibilities of incompletion that the others are. We can fail to interiorize, to accept values for our own. We may grow up respecting only external policemen. Many supposedly mature believers have been educated to ask a clergy-person to make their moral decisions. They slavishly follow the advice given. They have developed only a purely external conscience. Then there are those who consult only their own desires and develop only a purely internal conscience. A true conscience is one that seeks to be educated in moral matters and them makes its own moral decisions. The ability to make one's own decisions is a necessary part of the maturation process. It is an exercise that is vital to living a life of committed faith.

There are two concepts which, once established in the mind, regulate faith. There are the concepts of God and Self. When we think about it, there are two concepts which regulate the depth of any relationship. They are the concepts of the Other and that of Self. For example, we may think of ourselves as "with it" when we share the latest gossip or become sarcastic, but the fact of the matter is that our listeners will never want to be close to us. Their concept of us will be very negative. If they see dried blood under our fingernails they will never share their secrets with us.

Likewise, it is very important to the development of a healthy spirituality that I have an accurate and attractive concept of God. I have to pause for a moment to ask what is my concept or idea of

God. Is God more just than merciful? Does God have a mark book? Does God get angry or punish? Who was the God to whom I was first introduced? Who is the God of my guts?

If God does not love me and forgive my sins, as the psalmist says: "Who will endure it?" It might help to imagine the one person who is the most loving person you or I know. Then multiply the compassion, love and goodness of this person infinitely and we have a dim idea of what God is like.

The other concept which is difficult to get one's hands on is the concept of Self. Do I truly like myself? Would I change places with some other human being? Do I accept myself as a fraction: partly good and partly evil? Or am I an "all or nothing" kind of person? Such a person, if he or she tells one lie, assumes the identity of a "liar." This in spite of the fact that ninety-nine times out of a hundred, the person tells the truth. Or it may be that I am a perfectionist: nothing I do is ever good enough because I have not done it perfectly. If I set out to enjoy my life I probably will do a much better job of it then if I set out to be perfect. Perfectionism is a drain on the human spirit.

So these are the crises of faith. I know them well, because I have met them. I would like to say because I have "survived them," but at least for me they are an ongoing reality.

CHAPTER NINE

Faith and Prayer

It is almost a truism that the depth of every human relationship is determined by communication. Thomas Merton in an exhortation to his religious community once asked: "What is community?" He then proceeded to say that it was not the fact that we wear the same type of clothes or that we live in the same structure. It rather means that we have something in common. Only through real human communication with one another we discover that what we have in common is ourselves, our human persons.

*O*bviously, the communication of ourselves in faith is prayer. The person who does not pray well often does not believe very deeply. Communication involves both listening and speaking. It is reliably said that we listen with only twenty-five percent of our capacity. And in the matter of prayer, I would like to suggest that it is probably even less than this.

My personal experience of prayer suggests that there are five human antennae through which God communicates himself to us: They are *the mind, the will, the imagination, the emotions and the memory.* Let's take them in order. *The mind* we know gets ideas, makes judgments, reasons from one thing to another. I once asked a class of mine if God could put ideas into a mind. I was surprised that a student answered, "No, because that would deprive us of freedom." I responded to this student that as a teacher I was constantly proposing new ideas, launching new reasoning processes. But I knew then and I know now that the students were free to accept or reject these ideas and these reasoning processes.

I also remember responding to this student that, if God could not put ideas into our minds, I could see no logical reason for faith. Of course, it is no simple matter to distinguish my own ideas from those that are placed in my mind by God. It is so easy to deceive ourselves about the origin of the content of our prayer. The Time, Reality, Love tests mentioned earlier have to be applied here. The process when applied to prayer is called "discernment." Is God really speaking to me or have I just imagined it?

Most of us have experienced various types of "delusory" communication. At times we have been deceived. On the other hand, most of us have received some kind of communication from God. I remember once telling a class that on several occasions of my life, I heard words in my imagination that I felt confident were from God. As I walked out of the classroom, I heard one young man say to another, "I wish God spoke to me the way he does to Powell."

We were discussing *the mind,* as a contact point of God. The communication of prayer can put new ideas in the mind, new perspectives, new knowledge of self and of God, new inspirations or possibilities. Because of God's communication to our minds, we can see more and more clearly the meaning of life. Sometimes we can even understand purposes of God in allowing this individual person to suffer or the suffering of the whole human race.

God can also come to us through the antenna of *the will*. God can strengthen our wills to do things we never thought possible. God can inspire us with new desires, or give us the courage to go on. God can brace our wills to overcome persistent habits of human weakness. God can, through the infusion of grace into our wills, help us to commit ourselves to a deep and lasting love. We often speak of lacking the "will power" to do this or that. I recall wanting to quit smoking cigarettes. I tried everything, all the medical remedies, the psychological helps. I even doused a pack of cigarettes with water, in my white-hot fervor to quit. I later dried them out and smoked them.

Then one morning, I resorted to prayer. ("When all else fails, try prayer.") I poor mouthed God, told him I wanted to give up smoking, but had no lasting success. I just didn't have the strength of will. As I recall, the year was 1974, when God said to me: "I have the strength." "Okay, you've got the strength, but you have to give it to me." This was my transforming moment, like that of Bill Wilson. I never smoked again, nor even wanted to smoke.

When I realized what had happened, I went to the chapel, and said to the Lord, "You did it. Thank you." In reply (I'm not sure which of the channels God used), God said: "Oh, helping you to quit smoking is one of my minor jobs. I could do even greater things through you, but you are not ready yet." I thought about this for a long time. What I have concluded about my readiness for "other" graces is this: I had tried to quit smoking on my own. As the medical evidence piled up, I saw smoking as stupid. Yet, there was nothing I could do about it. When I finally turned to God, I came as a failure. I was ready to recognize the power of God. I knew what was meant when God said: "I have the strength."

The imagination. I am reminded of George Bernard Shaw's script on Joan of Arc. In the dialogue, Robert says to Joan: "Do you really hear the voice of God?" Joan replies: "Yes, I do." Robert thinks the whole thing is a delusion, and replies: "Oh, you hear only the voice of your imagination." So Joan says: "Yes, that is how God speaks to us."

The imagination has been defined as an "inner sense," one that can reduplicate within us the data of the exterior senses. For example, I can, by the use of my imagination, recall my Mother calling me in from play to practice the piano. Or I can sense again the sights and sounds of dinner cooking on the stove at the home of my childhood. God can also use this faculty or antenna to talk to me, to help me see the gentle face of the Lord, "to imagine" scenes from his life.

The emotions. Of course, God can reach us through our emotions or feelings. When we are emotionally bitter or discouraged, when we feel the dull aches of loneliness, God can transform these emotions by the gentle touch of his power and grace. God has not only effected physical cures in those open to Him, but emotional healing also. If God can make a leper clean, he can also make a neurotic normal. But the big thing is to give God all the initiative and let God keep it. I am nothing. God is everything.

The final channel of reception is *the memory.* As the poet Barrie once wrote: "We have memories so we can have roses in December." Perhaps you would not agree with me, but I think that at least half of what we are is determined by the memories which we carry inside us. When first I saw people praying over others for a healing of hurtful memories, I thought to myself that this is a good place to start. What the prayers seemed to say was this, that God alone can heal the memories that have flayed the person to rawness.

So God communicates to us through the memory. It has been said that the only real mistake is the one from which we have learned nothing. God communicates to us by stimulating in us a stored memory, calling to conscious and helpful awareness an event of the past. God can also stir up our love or prevent us from repeating an old mistake. In this way God can also remind us of an old lesson.

So it is through these channels we have the possibility of direct and immediate communication from God. However, to open ourselves to these communications we must learn to open these channels to God. We must slowly be introduced to the delicate vanishing art of listening. This demands of us a willingness to sit quietly at the feet of God. In the stillness of a living faith, we must learn to await the touch of God.

Please pardon a word of personal testimony. Over the years God seems to be straightening out the tangled perspectives of my mind, helping me to see with greater accuracy the important things in life. To some extent God has given me the ability to distinguish the important things in life from the unimportant. God has gradually enkindled in my will the desire to love and help others. I have also felt the touch of God's grace in my imagination. I have heard God say: "I love you. I am with you. I am counting on you." I have been transformed from an emotionally self-pitying person to a gratefully optimistic person. And so many times God has revived in me memories of this tenderness, strengthening me for the future by reminding me of his faithful help in the past. I have often thought that one of the reasons I know God loves me is that God has spared me from myself. My life could easily have ended in disaster.

Through this kind of interaction and dialogue with God, we gradually come to know both God and ourselves. Even though we start this search for God and self with massive false impressions, we will gradually attain a truer and clearer image of God and self.

Prayer, then, is a willingness to "level" with and listen to God. Once we have truly opened to God, with no clutched, concealing hands behind our backs, we will never be the same, or even seem to be the same. The deadliest delusion, of course, would be that God is not interested in me. Who could go on talking to a wall? These doubts will diminish when we have experienced successful communication with God at prayer.

I truly believe this: Whenever anything happens in my own life, I wonder what God is saying. I recently sat with a chaplain in a hospital. I asked him if God wasn't saying something, perhaps several things, through the spread of AIDS? He responded, "Oh no, I would never say this."

And yet, when one closes this door, you close down the question. Maybe God is saying this: "Be compassionate." Whatever the message, it is my opinion that God is saying something. As my own life unfolds, especially in major events, I wonder what God is saying through these happenings. How is God dealing with my mind and heart? As we listen and try to understand what God is saying, each of us will gradually develop a type of habitual awareness, an instinct for God. This is what I meant when earlier I wrote that faith is like putting on a new pair of glasses. Things look very different. We must learn to see through the eyes of faith. We must learn to discern patiently how God is at work in a situation. It is an acquired grace. We have to learn to listen to what God is saying. This, I think, is very important.

People who believe and pray are what attracts me personally to faith. They seem to be much more peaceful and in a deeper contact with reality. A woman like the late, great Mother Teresa, a man like Padre Pio, really defy explanation. They became who they were because of their faith in the Lord. C.S. Lewis once wrote that there are a lot of things that go into a general disposition. A person might be subject to headaches or have a faulty digestive tract. So you have to take the same person before and after faith. I know that, in my own life, I have been happier during the times I was closest to God.

This brings me to a difficulty, and it may well be good that my faith is tested. When I look out over a large crowd of human beings, say a hundred thousand or more, I am led to question whether God really has a plan for each, if God is really working in every one of them. Then I think of God's infinity. God's infinite goodness and patience. As the mountains gradually emerge from the ground, slowly my doubts tend to disappear.

CHAPTER TEN

Faith and Love

*God is love, and whoever lives in love
lives in union with God and God lives
in union with that person . . . There is
no fear in love; perfect love drives out
all fear. (1 John 4: 16–18)*

The thing that I have found most common in religious experience
is that God seems to enter a life when the person in question is
actively loving. I used to ask my classes if there were any religious
experiences among the students. On one occasion a tall (are there
any other kind?) basketball player stood up and announced to the
class that he had experienced God in an annual *Kairos* retreat.
(*Kairos* in Greek means "the hour." *Kairos Theou* means "the
hour of God.") He explained to the class that at the final exercise
the parents write a letter to the young person making the retreat.

Maybe for the first time they wear their hearts on their sleeves. They say how proud they are, how much they love the young person in question. It is at this point that the tears usually come. One Oriental boy, whose eyes were slanted of course, caused laughter in the class when he told us about his *Kairos* retreat. Apparently, he cried. "I tried to push the tears back but they kept coming out."

Once I was to give a sermon on the two disciples of Jesus on the road to Emmaus. You will recall that they did not recognize Jesus until "the breaking of the bread." I checked with a commentary on the gospels, and found that an interpretation I had always believed to be true was not even mentioned. I had always thought that the breaking of the bread was Holy Communion. Instead the commentary said that it wasn't until the two disciples were loving enough to ask the stranger to have dinner with them that they recognized the Lord.

But perhaps the most convincing example for me would be that of "Tommy." Tommy came into my class on the Theology of Faith, combing his long flaxen hair which was down to his wrists. I filed him under S for Strange. He turned out to be the resident atheist in my class. He questioned everything I said in a nasal, whiny voice. I secretly compared him to a case of "athlete's foot." Like the fungus, he didn't kill you but he drove you crazy.

When Tommy came up to turn in his final exam, he asked me in his whiny voice if I thought he would ever "find God." I have no idea why I turned to shock treatment at that moment, but I thundered: "NO!" Tommy was a bit taken back by this, so he countered: "I thought that was the product you were pushing." I felt all the emotions of impatience that I have projected into Jesus with the woman at the well. "No," I said, "I'm not pushing anything." I got a dull, unresponsive, "Oh..." I was convinced that my shock therapy did not work.

Then I heard that Tommy was sick. I thought of looking him up, but had almost decided against it, when he came in to see me. He now carried only one-hundred pounds on his six foot frame, and his hair was all gone, due to the chemotherapy. I greeted him in my office with: "Tommy, I heard you were sick."

"Oh yes, indeed I am sick. Sometimes I think I am just fooling people by breathing." Always fascinated by the study of death and dying, I urged him to tell me about it. He slouched down in my visitor's chair, and declined to talk about death. But he added, "I want to talk about the last day of class. Do you remember?" Of course I did remember. I had rehearsed it so many times in my own mind, always wondering where I had gone wrong.

After my nod that I did remember, Tommy opened up to me. "You had no way of knowing this, but I wasn't looking for God. I told God to wait in the wings of the stage until I called Him. God would just clutter up my life with a lot of silly rules. And there was money to be made, woman to be romanced, drinks to be drunk, songs to be sung. I laughed as I turned the corner and you could no longer see me.

"I started a business which was doing fairly well. Then surgeons took a lump out of me and told me it was cancerous, and that they would soon investigate as to whether it has spread. When I realized my life was at stake, I started to pray again. Soon the surgeon delivered the bad news: the cancer had spread. He promised me that he would soon begin chemotherapy, to try to kill the cancer cells that had spread throughout my body. I continued to try to call God out of the wings of the stage of my life. But God did not come.

"What I was doing was playing a 'trainer.' You know, 'C'mon, God, jump through my hoop. If the doctors are right, I have only months to live. But apparently, God is not a trained animal.

"Have you ever tried something for a long time, and then you got fed up because it did not work? That's how I felt about prayer. God, if God exists, was not interested in me, and I was not interested in God. So I reflected on something else you had once said in class. You told us about your father, how he kept a well-used sign over his feelings: 'Do not trespass!' You said that the saddest thing would be to go through life without loving, and the second saddest thing would be to go through life having loved, but never having shared this love.

"When you think of saying 'I love you' to another person, you worry about whether the feeling is mutual. But when you have a very limited amount of time to live, you just let it all hang out. What the hell? Why not?

"So I went to my father, the hardest nut of all to crack. He was hiding behind his newspaper as he does every night. 'Dad,' I said, 'I would like to talk to you.' He lowered the newspaper just low enough to see over the top of it, 'Well, talk!' 'Dad, I love you.' The newspaper fluttered slowly to the floor. And we talked, maybe for the first time, we talked. We went over the times I had smart-mouthed him, and the times he had grounded me. We apologized mutually and time flew by, through the whole night long. He shaved and went off to work, and I knew then and I know now that he truly cares.

"So, empowered by this success, I went to my little brother, and said to him: 'I know I teased you, called you names, wouldn't take you with me when I went out...but, I want you to know, I love you. We hugged and meant it for the first time, too.

"Then God was suddenly there. Apparently it is true that God found me, rather than I would find God. It seems to be true also that when you open the doors of your heart to love, God walks in through those open doors. Anyway, I want you to know that I'll be dying happy, because God and I are close again. As St. John once wrote: 'God is love, and whoever abides in love, abides in God, and God abides in him.'"

"Oh, Tommy," I gasped. "You were a big pain in the back pew when I had you in class, but you can make it all up to me now. Just come into my present theology of faith class and tell your story to them."

"Oh, wow! I was ready for you, but I don't really know if I am capable of facing your class. But I will let you know." He didn't make it, but at the hospital before he died, I did visit him. The last thing he said to me was: "You tell them for me. Will you?" So I have now told you, as I have told many people.

It just seemed very appropriate, in the discussion of faith and love, to re-tell it.

*I*n the gospel of *John* (Chapter 6) the following story is told. (Adapted . . .)

First Jesus decides to talk to his twelve apostles, but soon a large crowd collects around him. The gospel tells us that there were five thousand men, but it is well known that they did not count women. So I am presuming that there were about five thousand men and about an equal number of women and the children they were able to bring. Jesus does not fail them, but near the end of the day, he asks the apostles if "these people have had anything to eat?" How do you tell the Master that "You have been talking all day. How could they possibly have had anything to eat?" They politely demurred, with a shrug of the shoulders.

Then the most naive of all the apostles, Philip, comes forth with a small boy who has five loaves of bread and two fish. The other apostles give Philip that famous look. "Phil, you have just passed the sound barrier of naiveté." Jesus asks the boy if he wishes to give the loaves and the fish to feed the hungry crowd. The boy says it is okay with him, though like the apostles he can't see what good a mere pittance of loaves and fish will do.

So Jesus lines up the apostles, a food sack over the arm of each. He breaks up the fish and loaves and puts a small amount of fish and loaves in each sack. The apostles don't know what this whole thing is about, but they have learned not to question the Lord. Then he instructs them to line the people up in squares of about one hundred, so they will know who has been fed and who hasn't.

I myself delight in the picture of the twelve lining up more than ten thousand people on a hillside. "Oh, Kid, go find your mother." "No, Mrs. Goldberg, we want an aisle there." But finally it is achieved. The people are lined up.

So the distribution of the five loaves and two fish is about to begin. Again, I take great delight in imagining an apostle going to the first in line, the poor fellow sitting, as he was told. As the apostle leans down toward the poor man, he tells him to reach in and help himself. And the man comes up with loaves and fish in abundance. The apostle gives him a dirty look. He silently says: "You pig, that was all there was." Then he goes to the man's wife: "Help yourself, if there's any left." And she comes up with handsful of fish and loaves. Soon it is apparent. It is hard to fool Mrs. Goldfarb, sitting in the first row. "It is a MIRACLE."

After the people finish eating, it starts like a small rumble, but soon grows into a mass chant: "Be our KING." The poor apostles knew the centrality of the Kingdom in the preaching of Jesus. They begin cheerleading. "Give me a K . . . give me a I . . . give me a N . . . " They are ecstatic, until Jesus tells them to meet him on the other side of the lake. They mildly protest: "Do you hear what they are saying? They want you to be their king!"

But the Lord, who always seemed to know what he was doing, says, "Anchors Aweigh." And so the lonely apostles, who five minutes ago were riding on the highest crest, row across the lake. "The poor Lord is bad at timing. This was the hour to strike." As planned, Jesus meets them.

As the apostles saw it, it was fortunate that the people came too. The chant, "Be our King!" was still in the air. Then Jesus raises the hand that has just worked a miracle and fed them. The

Lord says, "Do you know why you want me to be your king? Because of the fish and loaves."

It was probably true. Others had delighted in "beating up the Jews." They were living, at the moment Jesus spoke, under the chafing rule of Rome. If he could multiply loaves and fish, he could also multiply swords and shields and chariots. He could throw off the heavy yoke of Rome.

So Jesus continues: "If you want to enter my kingdom, you have to *believe*. Faith in me and in my Father is the passport into my kingdom."

A man near the front challenges the Lord: "We are believers. Moses tested the faith of our forefathers in the journey across the desert. They had nothing to eat. But God gave them manna from heaven. We truly believe that. We are ready for any test of faith."

So Jesus rejoins, "You want your faith tested? Your forefathers ate the manna and they died, didn't they?" The large crowd of Jews standing around did not know where Jesus was headed. They looked a little bewildered, "Sure, they died. You know what they say about death and taxes." There was a ripple of laughter. Then the Lord tests their faith as it had never been tested before.

"I am the bread of life. If you eat this bread, you will never die." The Jews looked a little perplexed at this. They ask: "Would you run that one by us again?"

"Amen, amen I say this to you." (The *Amen* at the beginning was a sign of the importance of what he was about to say) "I am the bread of life. If you eat my Body and drink my blood, you will never die. You will live forever."

The reaction was strong. "What does he think we are: a bunch of cannibals? And who does he think he is?" The large crowd, which minutes before had been calling for Jesus to be their king, grumbling now, quietly disperses.

I am told, and I believe, that you do not know another person until you get a firm grasp on their feelings. Somehow the scene that follows, lays bare for me the inner feelings of Jesus. The apostles had been human yo-yos this day. First they were up and then they were down. They stand there, looking sad, as Jesus is losing his whole following. Peter, the one who always had footprints around his mouth, says for the whole group: "Lord, did you have to lay that one on them? It is definitely a hard saying."

It is then and in this remark that I can lay hold of the feelings of Jesus. He asks simply: "Do you want to go with them?" The question hangs on the twilight air, until Peter reassures the Lord.

"No, we can't go with them. You have the words that lead to life. Where could we possibly go if we left you?"

So it is. Faith remains the passport to the kingdom. Faith is a gift of God. Faith is the utter leap, the absolute paradox, the pearl of great price. Faith is like a new pair of glasses, through which everything looks different. Faith is so fragile and yet endures so many crises. Faith alone makes sense of life. Faith gives a person a reason to live and a reason to die. Faith alone explains our origin and destiny. All of us experience the human yo-yo feeling at times. But the question of the Lord remains, and our answer remains:

"Where could we possibly go if we left you?"

His books whisper to our souls—
bringing peace and purpose to our lives.

John Powell, professor of Theology at Loyola University in Chicago, is one of the foremost Christian authors of our time. He has academic degrees in The Classics (Latin and Greek), English, Philosophy, Psychology, and Theology. This native of Chicago has published nineteen books on theological and psychological themes.

Powell's books have more than fifteen million copies in circulation and have been listed by the American Library Association as among "the most significant books" published in U.S. history. Powell has received various journalism awards and is also widely recognized for his pro-life efforts. Recently, the Association for Religious and Values Issues in Counseling granted him its "Humanitarian Award."

Best-sellers by John Powell

Why Am I Afraid to Tell You Who I Am?
 Insights into self-awareness, personal growth, and
 honest communication.

✔ *Why Am I Afraid to Love?*
 Overcoming fears that limit our potential for enjoying love
 and life.

Fully Human, Fully Alive
 Faith, hope, and love make a person fully human and fully alive.

✔ *The Secret of Staying in Love*
 Communication is essentially an act of pure love and the secret
 of staying in love.

Happiness Is an Inside Job
 Ten life practices for attaining personal peace and satisfaction.

Touched by God
 Powell's own faith journey.

Through the Eyes of Faith
  To be holy is to be humanly whole.

Through Seasons of the Heart
  A book of inspirational readings for the entire year.

Will the Real Me Please Stand Up?
  Twenty-five basic attitudes and practices for effective
  human communication.

Abortion: The Silent Holocaust
  An eloquent and calming testimony to the value and sanctity of
  human life.

✓ *A Life-Giving Vision: How to Be a Christian in Today's World*
  How to really enjoy life and love and not waste one
  glorious opportunity.

Solving the Riddle of Self: The Search for Self-Discovery
  Practical steps to grow in self-knowledge and fulfillment.

✓ *Unconditional Love*
  Unconditional love is a permanent gift of the heart.